MW00641932

Guitar Chord Flipbook

An Essential Acoustic and Electric
Guitar Chord Reference Manual
that Fits in Your Guitar Case

MICAH BROOKS

PUBLISHING | EST. 1985

Also By Micah Brooks

The Guitar Authority Series

Worship Guitar In Six Weeks
A Complete Beginner's Guide to Learning Rhythm Guitar for Christian Worship Music

42 Guitar Chords Everyone Should Know
A Complete Step-By-Step Guide To Mastering 42 Of The Most Important Guitar Chords

Fast Guitar Chord Transitions
A Beginner's Guide to Moving Quickly Between Guitar Chords Like a Professional

Guitar Secrets Revealed
Unconventional and Amazing Guitar Chords, Professional Techniques, Capo Tricks, Alternate Tunings, Head Math, Rhythm & More

a!

!a

a!!

The Piano Authority Series

***Piano Chords One
(All Seven Natural Keys)***
*A Beginner's Guide To Simple Music Theory
and Playing Chords To Any Song Quickly*

***Piano Chords Two
(All Flat and Sharp Keys)***
*A Beginner's Guide To Simple Music Theory
and Playing Chords To Any Song Quickly*

Songbooks and Music

Micah Brooks All Things New EP Songbook

Micah Brooks All Things New EP

Christian Books

Forsaking All Others
The book we wish we'd had when dating, engaged, and in the early years of our marriage to set us up for future success.

21 Day Character Challenge
A Daily Devotional and Bible Reading Plan

Galatians
A Fresh, New Six Day Bible Study and Commentary

Ephesians
A Fresh, New Six Day Bible Study and Commentary

James
A Fresh, New Five Day Bible Study and Commentary

Micah Brooks

Copyright Information

Cover Design by Micah Brooks Kennedy

Dedication

It's an honor to dedicate this book to my three years I spent living in France as a young boy. I fell in love with the guitar and playing music during that season. I also learned just about every chord that is detailed for you in this book during that time as well. I appreciate now the influence that several guitarists had on me while we were expatriated. And lastly, I'm glad that my dad brought along his vintage Yamaha F-Series acoustic guitar and let me wear it out!

Table of Contents

Introduction

Welcome!

Thank you for purchasing the one and only *Guitar Chord Flipbook*. A flipbook is intentionally small and made to travel with you. Keep this in your guitar case, notebook, or gig bag. You never know when you'll need the step by step directions for how to play a unique chord that a song requires. This manual is ready to serve this exact purpose.

Chord Diagram

Each chord in this book has a unique diagram. There are several parts to each one. Refer back to this section as you need to when working through this manual.

Chord Diagram Explained

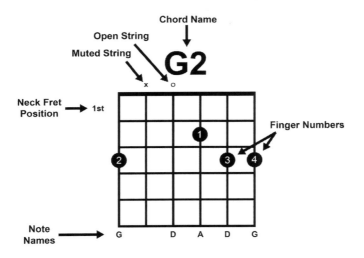

Chord Name

This section gives you the name of the chord. This may include a chord suffix, like G2 where the "2" is at the end and is a modifier.

Open String

An open string is a guitar string that is played with no finger touching it. The note name is the string's name. For example, if you play an open fourth string (like in this G2 chord example), the open note being played on the D string (4) is a "D". An open string will always have an "o" above the string.

Muted String

A muted string is one that is either being muted by a neighboring finger or intentionally not being played with the right, strumming hand. In this example of the G2 chord, the A string (5) is not played. A muted string will always have an "x" above the string.

Neck Fret Position

The neck fret position number is important to always notice when reviewing a chord diagram. That number signifies the starting position of your fingers on the guitar neck. It can go as high as the last fret on the upper part of your guitar neck. If you see a "1st" denotation, then the chord is played in open position at the beginning of the neck. "1st" is the *home base* position on the guitar. Everything else is related to that home base position. Were you to see "5th", like in a D#m7 chord, then your root note begins on the sixth fret. Do your best to observe the neck fret position indication for each chord.

Finger Numbers

While you could use nicknames for each finger on your left hand (like your index finger, pinky, etc.) most guitar teachers will use numbers per finger. Using numbers allows for quick reference for chord diagrams and transitioning.

Here is how I detail each finger of the left hand. The index finger is (1). Your middle finger is (2), ring finger is (3), and pinky finger is (4). I label the thumb (T). While you will not get into any thumb playing in this book, you may as you improve in your skills moving on to further chording. Note: left-handed guitarists will use the opposite hand, making each of the labels above true for the *right hand* rather than your left.

Note Names

Below each chord diagram are the note names being played per string. Please notice that these are <u>not</u> the root names of the strings. Rather, these are the notes being played after fretting the chord. Some of the notes will be the open string notes, but only when there is no finger needed for that particular string in the chord. When a string is being omitted or muted, no note name will be present.

It's time to dive in! Let's go!

G

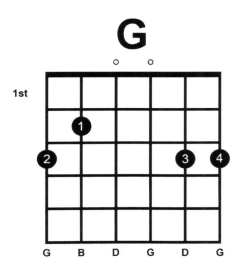

Step by Step Fingering Instructions

Place your index (1) finger on the second fret of the fifth [A] string. Follow with your middle (2) finger on the third fret of the sixth [E] string. Last, add your ring (3) and pinky (4) fingers to the third frets of both the second [B] and first [e] strings, respectively. Those final fingers should be tight fitting. Strum across all six strings and you will have a G chord.

Gm

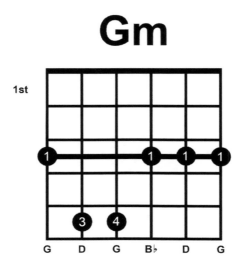

Step by Step Fingering Instructions

First, lay your index (1) finger across all six
strings on the third fret. Then add your ring (3)
and pinky (4) finger to the fifth frets of the fifth
[A] and fourth [D] strings, respectively. Once in
place, you should be able to strum across all six
strings to produce a Gm chord. It is important
that you hear the third fret note on the third [G]
string. As in the other six string minor chords,
that third fret note is what is making the Gm a
minor chord and not major.

Gm7

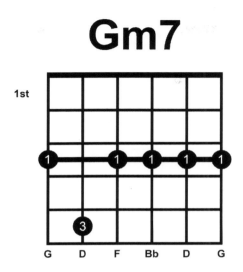

Step by Step Fingering Instructions

Lay your index (1) finger across all six strings on the third fret. Then only add your ring (3) finger to the fifth fret of the fifth [A] string. Once in place, you should be able to strum across all six strings to produce a Gm7 chord. It is important that you hear the third fret note on the third [G] string. As in the other six string minor chords, that third fret note is what is making the Gm7 a minor chord.

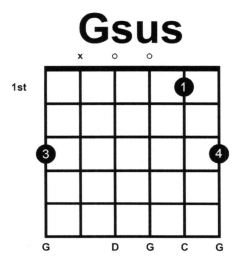

Step by Step Fingering Instructions

Begin by simultaneously placing your ring (3) finger on the third fret of the sixth [E] string and index (1) finger on the first fret of the second [B] string. It's important to add both of those fingers at the same time to create the chord shape quickly. Last, add your pinky (4) finger to the third fret of the first (e) string. Strum across all six strings to make a Gsus. Notice that your ring (3) finger will gently rest on the fifth [A] string which should mute that string.

G2

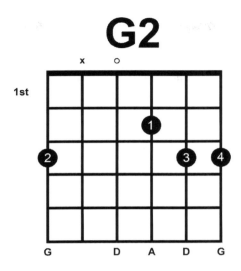

Step by Step Fingering Instructions

Place your index (1) finger on the second fret of the third [G] string. Next, add your middle (2) finger on the third fret of the sixth [E] string. Last, add your ring (3) and pinky (2) fingers to the third frets of both the second [B] and first [e] strings, respectively. Those fingers should fit tightly together. Your middle (2) finger should lightly touch the fifth [A] string to mute it. This is important. Strum all six strings, omitting the fifth [A] string to form a G2.

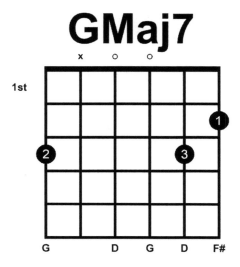

Step by Step Fingering Instructions

Place your middle (2) finger onto the third fret of the sixth [E] string. Next, add your ring (3) finger to the third fret of the second [B] string. Finally, reach your index (1) finger across the fret board to the second fret of the first [e] string. As with other chords, use your middle (2) finger to mute the fifth [A] string by lightly laying it on that string while keeping a tight hold of the third fret of the sixth [E] string. Strum all six strings, though you will be muting the fifth [A] string. Make sure that you hear the first [e] string ringing out. That is the "Maj7" note of GMaj7.

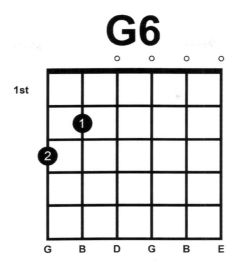

Step by Step Fingering Instructions

Begin by placing your index (1) finger on the second fret of the fifth [A] string. Last, add your middle (2) finger on the third fret of the sixth [E] string. Strum all six strings. Note that the first [e] string being open is what is creating the "6" in a G6. Make sure that you can hear that note when you strum this chord.

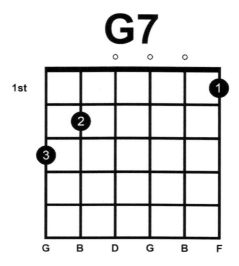

Step by Step Fingering Instructions

This chord frets similarly to a C chord. First, simultaneously place your ring (3) finger and your middle (2) finger onto the third fret of the sixth [E] string and second fret of the fifth [A] strings respectively. Last, add your index (1) finger to the first fret of the first (e) string. Strum across all six strings to sound a G7.

G# (A♭)

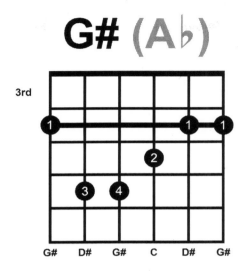

Step by Step Fingering Instructions

Begin by playing your index (1) finger across all six strings on the fourth fret. Then add your ring (3) and pinky (4) fingers on the sixth frets of the fifth [A] and fourth [D] strings. Last, place your middle (2) finger onto the fifth fret of the third [G] string. Strum all six strings. Practice this chord to increase strength. Another way to say G# is A♭.

G#m (A♭m)

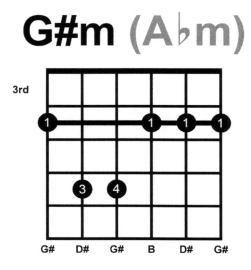

3rd

G# D# G# B D# G#

Step by Step Fingering Instructions

To begin, lay your index (1) finger across all six strings on the fourth fret. Next, add your ring (3) and pinky (4) fingers to the sixth frets of the fifth [A] and fourth [D] strings, respectively. Strum all six strings. It is important to make sure that the third [G] string can be heard while pressing down the fourth fret with your index (1) finger. That note is the *minor* note of the G#m (A♭m) chord. The other name for G#m is A♭m.

G#m7 (A♭m7)

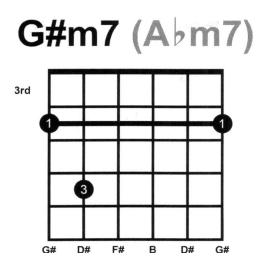

Step by Step Fingering Instructions

Begin by laying your index (1) finger across all six strings on the fourth fret. Next, add your ring (3) finger to the sixth fret of the fifth [A] string. Strum all six strings. It is important to make sure that the third [G] string can be heard while pressing down the fourth fret with your index (1) finger. That note is the *minor* note of the G#m7 chord. Your index (1) finger is also making the 7 note sound in this G#m7 on the fourth fret of the fourth [D] string. Be careful to make sure you hear each note of this six string barre chord. The other name for G#m7 is A♭m7.

25

G#sus (A♭sus)

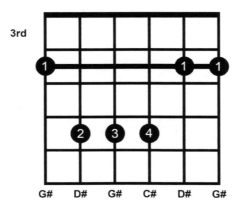

3rd

G#   D#   G#   C#   D#   G#

Step by Step Fingering Instructions

Begin by playing your index (1) finger across all six strings on the fourth fret. Then add your middle (2), ring (3), and pinky (4) fingers on the sixth frets of the fifth [A], fourth [D], and third [G] strings. Strum all six strings. Practice this chord to increase strength. Another name for G#sus is A♭sus.

26

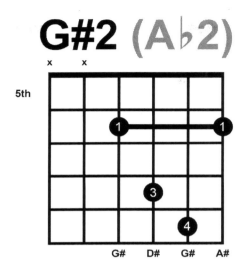

Step by Step Fingering Instructions

Begin this chord by placing your index (1) finger across the sixth fret beginning on the fourth [D] string to the first (e) string. Omit the bottom sixth [E] and fifth [A] strings. Next, add your ring (3) finger to the eighth fret of the third [G] string. Last, add your pinky (4) finger to the ninth fret of the second [B] string. Strum the last four strings. Please notice that the first (e) string's note, A#, on the sixth fret is the "2" note of the chord. You need to be able to hear that note when strumming across those four strings. Another name for G#2 is Ab2.

G#Maj7 (A♭Maj7)

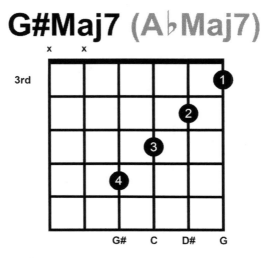

3rd

G#   C   D#   G

Step by Step Fingering Instructions

Begin by placing your pinky (4) finger onto the sixth fret of the fourth [D] string. As close to one motion as possible, attempt to place these fingers in this order at the same time: ring (3) finger on the fifth fret of the third [G] string; middle (2) finger on the fourth fret of the second [B] string; index (1) finger on the third fret of the first [e] string. Strum only the last four strings. Another name for G#Maj7 is A♭Maj7.

G#6 (A♭6)

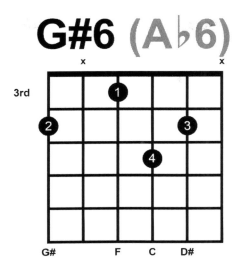

Step by Step Fingering Instructions

Begin by placing your index (1) finger on the third fret of the fourth [D] string. Next, add your middle (2) finger to the fourth fret of the sixth [E] string. Following, add your ring (3) finger to the fourth fret of the second [B] string. Finally, stretch your ring (4) finger to the fifth fret of the third [G] string. Allow your middle (2) and ring (3) fingers to lightly touch the fifth [A] and first [e] strings, respectively. This will mute those strings. Strum across all six strings to create the sound of G#6, also known as A♭6.

G#7 (A♭7)

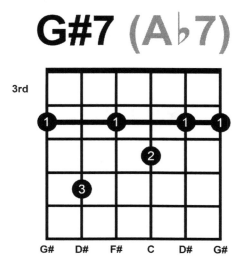

3rd

G# D# F# C D# G#

Step by Step Fingering Instructions

Start by laying your index (1) finger across all six strings on the fourth fret. Now add your ring (3) finger onto the sixth fret of the fifth [A] string. Finally, place your middle (2) finger onto the fifth fret of the third [G] string. Strum across all six strings. It is important to hear the F# note played on the fourth [D] string. This is the 7 note in G#7. Another name for G#7 is A♭7.

A

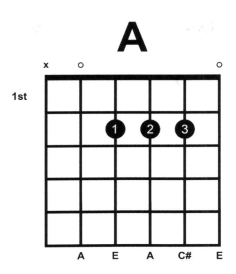

Step by Step Fingering Instructions

Begin by placing your index (1) finger on the second fret of the fourth [D] string. Continue by placing your middle (2) finger on the second fret of the third [G] string. Last, place your ring (3) finger on the second fret of the second [B] string. Strum the last five strings, omitting the low [E] string. You need to practice getting into this position often, as muscle memory will develop.

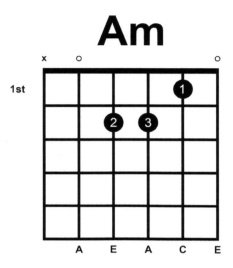

Step by Step Fingering Instructions

Start by placing the index (1) finger on the first fret of the second [B] string. Then add your middle (2) finger to the second fret of the fourth [D] string. Last, add your ring (3) finger to the second fret of the third [G] string. You may be noticing the tight squeeze of all three fingers close together. This is normal. With good upright pressure with your left hand, all three fingers will fit into their proper place. Strum only the bottom five strings to make an Am.

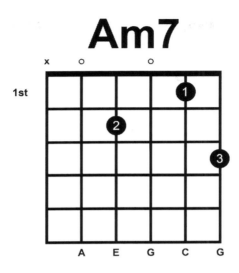

Step by Step Fingering Instructions

First, place your index (1) finger on the first fret of the second [B] string. Then add your middle (2) finger to the second fret of the fourth [D] string. Last, add your ring (3) finger to the third fret of the first [e] string. Adding the third finger may be a stretch for you. Do your best to practice this chord often and you will get better at making that stretch. Strum only the last five strings to form an Am7.

Asus

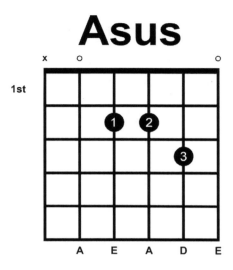

Step by Step Fingering Instructions

Begin by placing your index (1) finger onto the second fret of the fourth [D] string. Next, add your middle (2) finger on the second fret of the third [G] string. The final step is to place your ring (3) finger on the third fret of the second [B] string. Those fingers should fit tightly together. Strum only the last five strings to form the Asus chord.

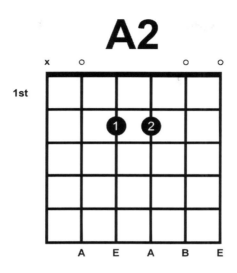

Step by Step Fingering Instructions

Place your index (1) finger on the second fret of the fourth [D] string. Follow that with your middle (2) finger on the second fret of the third [G] string. Those fingers should fit tightly together. Strum only the last 5 strings to make the A2.

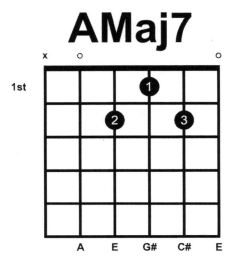

Step by Step Fingering Instructions

Begin by placing your middle (2) finger on the second fret of the fourth [D] string. Next, add your index (1) finger to the first fret of the third [G] string. The final step is to place your ring (3) finger on the second fret of the second [B] string. Note that your fingers will be in a tight package. Strum only the last five strings to sound AMaj7.

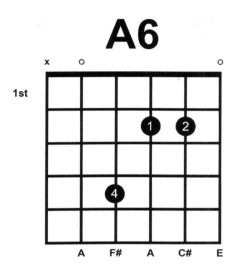

Step by Step Fingering Instructions

Begin by placing your index (1) finger on the second fret of the third [G] string. Next, add your middle (2) finger on the second fret of the second [B] string. Last, stretch your pinky (4) finger to the fourth fret of the fourth [D] string. Strum only the last five strings.

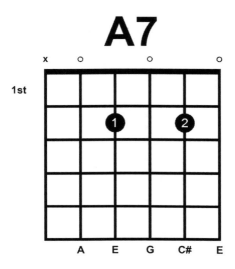

Step by Step Fingering Instructions

Start by placing your index (1) finger onto the second fret of the fourth [D] string. The only other finger to use in this chord is your middle (2) finger on the second fret of the second [B] string. Strum the last five strings, omitting the low [E] string. Notice that the third [G] string is open and not being touched by any fingers. This needs to be true to create the "7" in the A7. This may sound rather *twangy*.

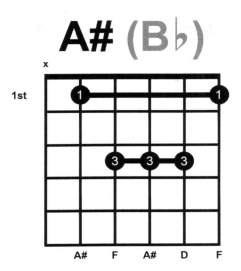

Step by Step Fingering Instructions

Begin by placing your index (1) finger on the first fret across the last five strings, omitting the sixth [E] string. Next, take your ring (3) finger and barre the third fret of the fourth [D], third [G], and second [B] strings. It is important that you do not cover up the first [e] string that the index (1) finger is currently pressing down on the first fret. Strum only the last five strings, omitting the sixth [E] string to play A#. Another name for A# is B♭.

A#m (B♭m)

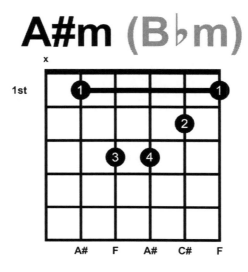

x

1st

A#   F   A#   C#   F

Step by Step Fingering Instructions

Begin by placing your index (1) finger as flat as you can across the first fret of all five strings beginning at the fifth [A] string. Omit the sixth [E] string for this chord. Next, add your middle (2) finger to the second fret of the second [B] string. Last, add your ring (3) finger and your pinky (4) finger to the third frets of the fourth [D] and third [G] strings, respectively. Once all fingers are in place you will strum the last five strings, leaving out the sixth [E] string. Another name for A#m is B♭m.

A#m7 (B♭m7)

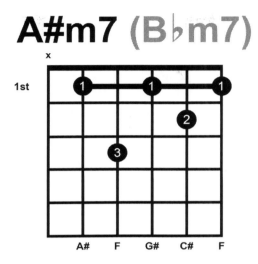

1st

A#   F   G#   C#   F

Step by Step Fingering Instructions

Start by placing your index (1) finger as flat as you can across the first fret of all five strings beginning at the fifth [A] string. Omit the sixth [E] string. Next, add your middle (2) finger to the second fret of the second [B] string. Finally, add your ring (3) finger to the third frets of the fourth [D] string. Once all fingers are in place you will strum the last five strings, leaving out the sixth [E] string. The other name for A#m7 is B♭m7.

A#sus (B♭sus)

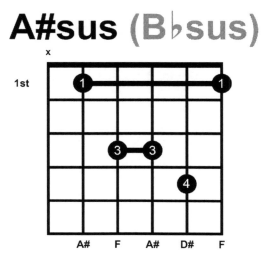

Step by Step Fingering Instructions

Start by placing your index (1) finger on the first fret across the last five strings, omitting the sixth [E] string. Next, take your ring (3) finger and barre the third fret of the fourth [D] and third [G] strings. Last, place your pinky (4) finger on the fourth fret of the second [B] string. Strum only the last five strings, omitting the sixth [E] string to play A#sus. The other name for A#sus is B♭sus.

42

A#2 (Bb2)

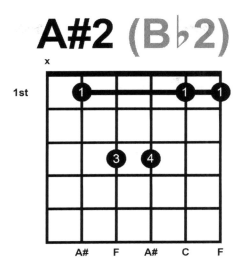

Step by Step Fingering Instructions

Start by placing your index (1) finger on the first fret across the last five strings, omitting the sixth [E] string. Next, place your ring (3) and pinky (4) fingers on the third frets of the fourth [D] and third [G] strings, respectively. Strum only the last five strings, omitting the sixth [E] string to play A#. Another name for A#2 is Bb2.

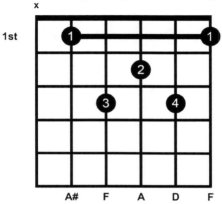

Step by Step Fingering Instructions

First, lay your index (1) finger across the first fret of the last five strings. This should be a strong barre in order to hear both the fifth [A] and first [e] strings being held down after you finish positioning each finger for this chord. Next, add your ring (3) finger onto the third fret of the fourth [D] string. Then add your middle (2) finger to the second fret of the third [G] string. Finally, add your pinky (4) finger to the third fret of the second [B] string. Strum only the last five strings to produce A#Maj7. The other name for this chord is B♭Maj7.

A#6 (B♭6)

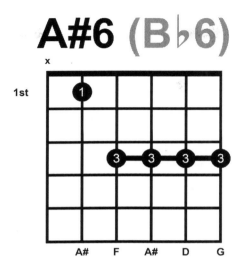

Step by Step Fingering Instructions

Begin by placing your index (1) finger on the first fret of the fifth [A] string. Last, barre your ring (3) finger across the third frets of the fourth [D], third [G], second [B], and first [e] strings. Your ring (3) finger may be tough to keep in place at first. Practice makes this chord perfect. Strum across only the last five strings. Another name for A#6 is B♭6.

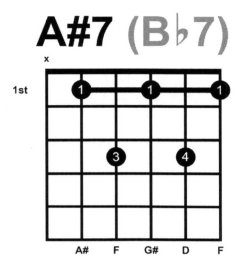

A#7 (B♭7)

Step by Step Fingering Instructions

To begin, lay your index (1) finger across the first fret of the last five strings. This should be a strong barre in order to hear both the fifth [A] and first [e] strings being held down after you finish positioning each finger for this chord. Next, add your ring (3) finger onto the third fret of the fourth [D] string. Last, add your pinky (4) finger to the third fret of the second [B] string. Strum only the last five strings to produce A#7. Another name for this chord is B♭7.

B

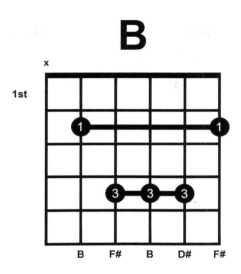

Step by Step Fingering Instructions

Begin by placing your index (1) finger on the second fret across the bottom five strings, omitting the sixth [E] string. Before we start the second barre, it is important that you have formed a strong hold, pressing firmly down on the second fret. Once in place, take your ring (3) finger and barre the fourth fret of the fourth [D], third [G], and second [B] strings. It is also important that you do not cover up the first [e] string that the index (1) finger is currently pressing down on the second fret. Strum the last five strings, omitting the sixth [E] string.

47

Bm

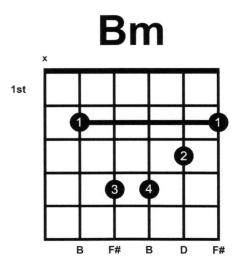

Step by Step Fingering Instructions

Begin by placing your index (1) finger as flat as you can across the second fret of all five strings beginning at the fifth [A] string on to the first [e] string. You can omit the sixth [E] string for this chord. Next, add your middle (2) finger to the third fret of the second [B] string. Confirm that your barre has not lost its strength. Last, add your ring (3) finger and your pinky (4) finger to the fourth frets of the fourth [D] and third [G] strings, respectively. Once all fingers are in place you will strum the last five strings, leaving out the sixth [E] string.

Bm7

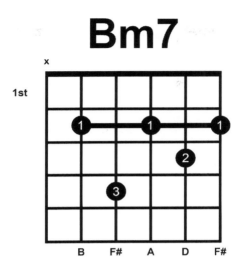

Step by Step Fingering Instructions

Start by placing your index (1) finger as flat as you can across the second fret of all five strings beginning at the fifth [A] string on to the first [e] string. You can omit the sixth [E] string for this chord. Next, add your middle (2) finger to the third fret of the second [B] string. Confirm that your barre has not lost its strength. Last, add your ring (3) finger to the fourth frets of the fourth [D] string. Once all fingers are in place you will strum the last five strings, leaving out the sixth [E] string to make Bm7.

Bsus

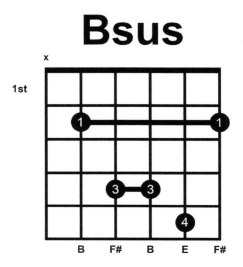

Step by Step Fingering Instructions

Begin by placing your index (1) finger on the second fret across the bottom five strings, omitting the sixth [E] string. Next, take your ring (3) finger and barre the fourth fret of the fourth [D] and third [G] strings. Add your pinky (4) finger to the fifth fret of the second [B] string. It is also important that you do not cover up the first [e] string that the index (1) finger is currently pressing down on the second fret. Strum the last five strings, omitting the sixth [E] string to form Bsus.

B2

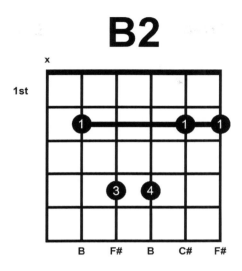

Step by Step Fingering Instructions

Begin by placing your index (1) finger on the second fret across the bottom five strings, omitting the sixth [E] string. Last, add your ring (3) and pinky (4) fingers to the fourth frets of the fourth [D] and third [G] strings, respectively. Strum only the last five strings to produce a B2 chord.

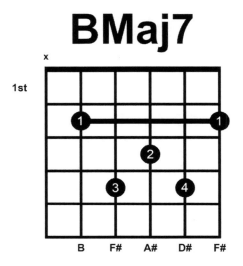

BMaj7

Step by Step Fingering Instructions

First, barre across the second frets of the fifth [A] to the first [e] strings. This is the base positioning for this chord. Next, add these fingers in order: First, add your ring (3) finger to the fourth fret of the fourth (D) string. Next, add your middle (2) finger to the third fret of the third (G) string. Finally, place your pinky (4) finger to the fourth fret of the second [B] string. Play only the last five strings to produce a BMaj7 chord.

B6

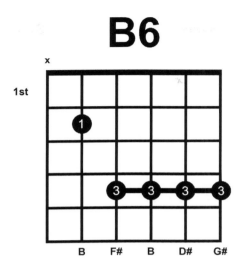

Step by Step Fingering Instructions

Start by placing your index (1) finger on the second fret of the fifth [A] string. Next, barre your ring (3) finger across the fourth frets of the fourth [D], third [G], second [B], and first [e] strings. Strum across only the last five strings to play B6.

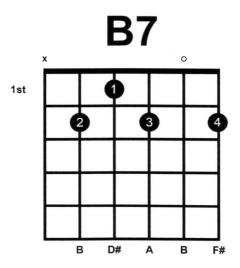

Step by Step Fingering Instructions

Start by placing your middle (2) finger on the second fret of the fifth [A] string. Next, add your index (1) finger to the first fret of the fourth [D] string. Place your ring (3) finger on the second fret of the third [G] string. Last, and this is a stretch for this finger, place your pinky (4) on the second fret of the first [e] string. Note that your fingers will feel like they are going in several directions. Strum the bottom five strings for this B7.

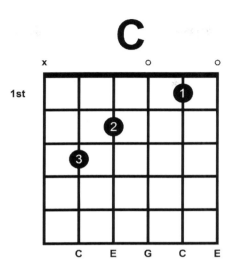

Step by Step Fingering Instructions

Begin by placing the index (1) finger on the first fret of the second [B] string. Make sure you make strong contact with that string without muting the third [G] and first [e] strings around it. Next, add your middle (2) finger to the second fret of the fourth [D] string. Finally, add your ring finger (3) to the third fret of the fifth [A] string. Strum across the last five strings, muting or not strumming the sixth [E] string to make the C chord.

Cm

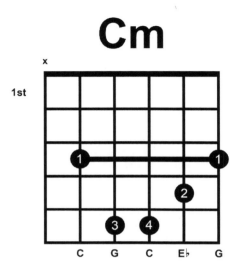

Step by Step Fingering Instructions

Start by taking your index (1) finger laying it at as flat as you can across the third fret of all five strings beginning at the fifth [A] string all to the way to the first [e] string. Next, add your middle (2) finger onto the fourth fret of the second [B] string. Last, add your ring (3) finger and your pinky (4) finger to the fifth frets of the fourth [D] and third [G] strings, respectively. Once all fingers are in place you will strum the last five strings, leaving out the sixth [E] string that is not being pressed down to make a Cm.

Cm7

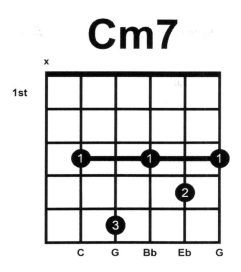

Step by Step Fingering Instructions

Begin by placing your index (1) finger as flat as you can across the third fret of all five strings beginning at the fifth [A] string all to the way to the first [e] string. Omit the sixth [E] string. Next, add your middle (2) finger onto the fourth fret of the second [B] string. Last, add your ring (3) finger to the fifth fret of the fourth [D] string. Once all fingers are in place you will strum only the last five strings, leaving out the sixth [E] string that is not being pressed down to make a Cm7.

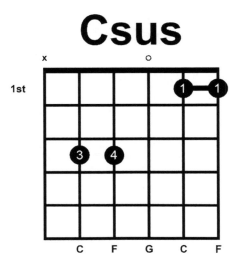

Step by Step Fingering Instructions

Begin by creating a two string barre on the first frets of the second [B] and first [e] strings with your index (1) finger. Next, add your ring (3) and pinky (4) fingers to the third frets of the fifth (A) and fourth (D) strings, respectively. Strum across only the bottom five strings to produce a Csus chord.

C2

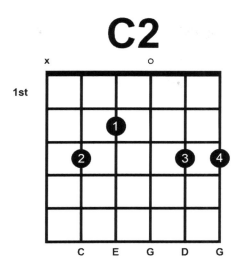

Step by Step Fingering Instructions

To begin, place your index (1) finger onto the second fret of the fourth [D] string. Next, add your middle (2) finger to the third fret of the fifth [A] string. Continue by placing your ring (3) and pinky (4) fingers on the third frets of the second [B] and first [e] strings, respectively. Strum only the last five strings, omitting the sixth [E] string to play C2. This chord is also known as Cadd9.

CMaj7

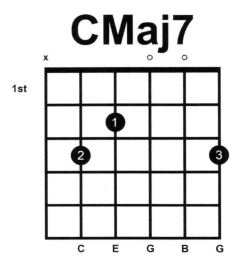

1st

C   E   G   B   G

Step by Step Fingering Instructions

First, add your middle (2) finger onto the third fret of the fifth [A] string. Next, add your index (1) finger to the second fret of the fourth [D] string. Last, add your ring (3) finger to the third fret of the first [e] string. Strum only the last five strings, always omitting the sixth [E] string. The open note on the second [B] string is what causes the "Maj7" sound in this chord. Confirm you can hear this note in your chord. Also, you can leave the first [e] string open instead of placing your ring (3) finger onto the third fret. Both are versions of a CMaj7 chord.

C6

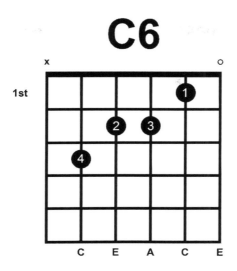

Step by Step Fingering Instructions

Start by placing the index (1) finger on the first fret of the second [B] string. Then add your middle (2) finger to the second fret of the fourth [D] string. Next, add your ring (3) finger to the second fret of the third [G] string. Last, place your pinky (4) finger on the third fret of the fifth [A] string. All four fingers should make a tight package. With good up and down pressure and zero left to right slouching, all four fingers will fit in their proper places. Strum only the bottom five strings to form C6.

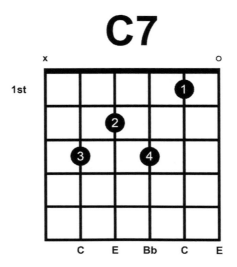

Step by Step Fingering Instructions

Begin by placing the index (1) finger on the first fret of the second [B] string. Then add your middle (2) finger to the second fret of the fourth [D] string. Next, add your ring finger (3) to the third fret of the fifth [A] string. Last, add your pinky (4) finger to the third fret of the third [G] string. These four fingers will sit together as a tight package. Strum C7 using only the last five strings, muting or not strumming the sixth [E] string.

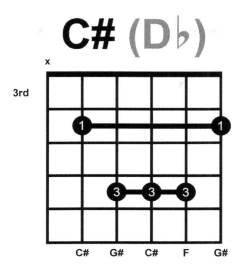

C# (Db)

Step by Step Fingering Instructions

Begin by placing your index (1) finger on the fourth fret across the bottom five strings, omitting the sixth [E] string. Next, take your ring (3) finger and barre the sixth fret of the fourth [D], third [G], and second [B] strings. It is also important that you do not cover up the first [e] string that the index (1) finger is currently pressing down on the second fret. Strum only the last five strings, omitting the sixth [E] string. Another name for C# is Db.

C#m (D♭m)

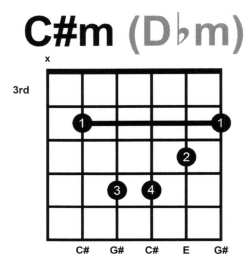

3rd

C# G# C# E G#

Step by Step Fingering Instructions

Begin by laying your index finger (1) as flat as you can across the fourth fret of all five strings, beginning at the fifth [A] string all the way across to the first [e] string. Next, add your middle (2) finger to the fifth fret of the second [B] string. Last, add your ring (3) and your pinky (4) fingers to the sixth frets of the fourth [D] and third [G] strings, respectively. Once all fingers are in place, you will only strum the last five strings, leaving out the sixth [E] string that is not being pressed down. The chord names C#m and D♭m are one and the same.

C#m7 (D♭m7)

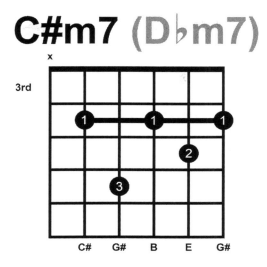

3rd

C# G# B E G#

Step by Step Fingering Instructions

Begin by laying your index (1) finger as flat as you can across the fourth fret of the last five strings. Omit the sixth [E] string for this chord. Next, add your middle (2) finger to the fifth fret of the second [B] string. Last, add your ring (3) finger to the sixth fret of the third [G] string. Strum only the last five strings. The chord names C#m7 and D♭m7 are one and the same.

C#sus (D♭sus)

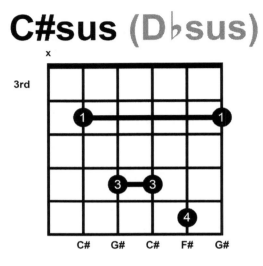

Step by Step Fingering Instructions

Begin by placing your index (1) finger as a barre across the last five strings on the fourth fret. Next, barre the sixth frets of the fourth [D] and third [G] strings with your ring (3) finger. Last, place your pinky (4) finger onto the seventh fret of the second [B] string. Strum only the last five strings. Another name for C#sus is D♭sus.

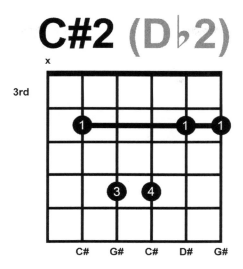

Step by Step Fingering Instructions

Place your index (1) finger as a barre on the fourth fret of the fifth [A] to first [e] strings. Simultaneously place your ring (3) and pinky (4) fingers onto the sixth frets of the fourth [D] and third [G] strings. Strum only the last five strings. Another name for C#2 is Db2.

C#Maj7 (D♭Maj7)

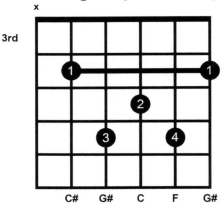

Step by Step Fingering Instructions

Begin by barring the fourth fret of fifth [A] string to the first [e] string. Next, add your ring (3) finger to the sixth fret of the fourth [D] string. Next, add your middle (2) finger to the fifth fret of the third [G] string. Finally, add your pinky (4) finger to the sixth fret of the second [B] string. Strum only the last five strings. Another name for C#Maj7 is D♭Maj7.

C#6 (D♭6)

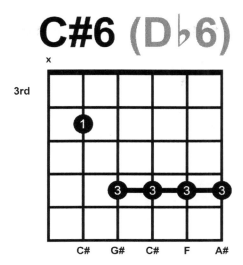

3rd

C# G# C# F A#

Step by Step Fingering Instructions

Begin by placing your index (1) finger on the fourth fret of the fifth [A] string. Last, barre your ring (3) finger across the sixth frets of the fourth [D], third [G], second [B], and first [e] strings. Your ring (3) finger may be difficult to keep in place at first. Practice makes this chord perfect. Strum across only the last five strings. Another name for C#6 is D♭6.

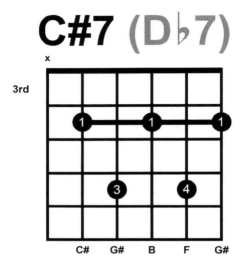

C#7 (D♭7)

Step by Step Fingering Instructions

Begin by laying your index (1) finger across the fourth fret of the last five strings. This should be a strong barre in order to hear both the fifth [A] and first [e] strings being held down after you finish positioning each finger for this chord. Next, add your ring (3) finger onto the sixth fret of the fourth [D] string. Last, add your pinky (4) finger to the sixth fret of the second [B] string. Strum only the last five strings to produce C#7. Another name for this chord is D♭7.

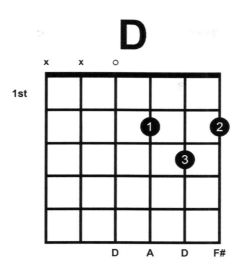

Step by Step Fingering Instructions

Begin by placing your index (1) finger on the second fret of the third [G] string. Add your middle (2) finger to the second fret of the first [e] string. Last, add your ring (3) finger to the third fret of the second [B] string. Strum only the bottom four strings to play D. Make sure you omit the sixth [E] and fifth [A] strings when you strum this chord.

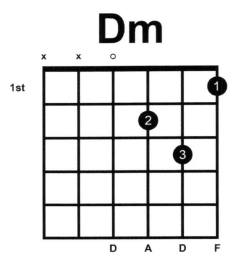

Step by Step Fingering Instructions

Start by placing your middle (2) finger on the second fret of the third [G] string. Add the ring (3) finger to the third fret of the second [B] string. Finally, put your index (1) finger onto the first fret of the first [e] string. Once in place, strum the last four strings. The top note that your index (1) finger is playing is the note that makes the chord a *minor*. Make sure that you hear that note when you strum all four strings.

Dm7

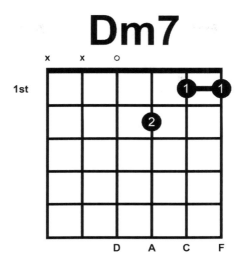

Step by Step Fingering Instructions

First, barre your index (1) finger on the first frets of the second [B] and first [e] strings. Last, add your middle (2) finger on the second fret of the third [G] string. Strum the last four strings to produce a Dm7 chord.

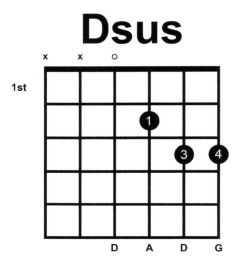

Step by Step Fingering Instructions

Begin by placing your index (1) finger on the second fret of the third [G] string. Then add your ring (3) finger to the third fret of the second [B] string. The final step is to add your pinky (4) finger to the third fret of the first [e] string. Strum only the last four strings. Special Note: The Dsus chord transitions quickly to the D chord. You only need to take off your pinky (4) finger from the first [e] string replacing it with your middle (2) finger on the second fret of the same first [e] string.

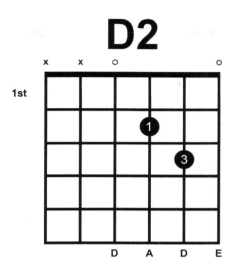

Step by Step Fingering Instructions

The first of two steps is to place your index (1) finger onto the second fret of the third [G] string. Last, add your ring (3) finger to the third fret of the second [B] string. Strum only the last four strings.

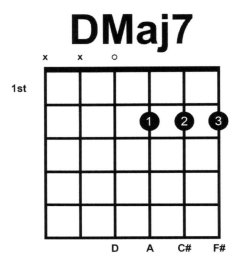

Step by Step Fingering Instructions

Begin by placing your index (1) finger on the second fret of the third [G] string. Next, add your middle (2) finger to the second fret of the second [B] string. Last, place your ring (3) finger onto the second fret of the first [e] string. Strum only the last four strings. The key to playing this chord correctly is all three fingers forming as tight of package as possible.

D6

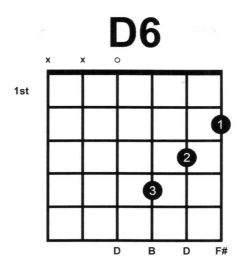

1st

x   x   o

D   B   D   F#

Step by Step Fingering Instructions

First, place your ring (3) finger onto the fourth fret of the third [G] string. Next, add your middle (2) finger to the third fret of the second [B] string. Last, add your index (1) finger to the second fret of the first [e] string. Strum only the last four strings to produce a D6 chord.

D7

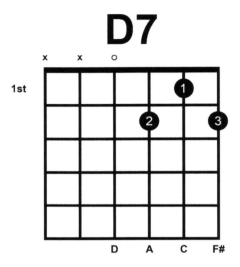

Step by Step Fingering Instructions

First, place your middle (2) finger on the second   index (1) finger on the first fret of the second [B] string. Finally, add your ring (3) finger to the second fret of the first [e] string. Only strum the last four strings to create a D7.

D# (E♭)

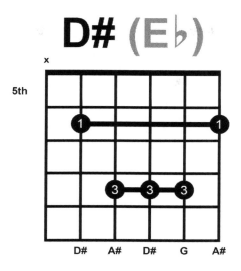

Step by Step Fingering Instructions

Begin by placing your index (1) finger on the sixth fret across the last five strings, omitting the sixth [E] string. Next, take your ring (3) finger and barre the eighth fret of the fourth [D], third [G], and second [B] strings. It is important that you do not cover up the first [e] string that the index (1) finger is currently pressing down on the sixth fret. Strum only the last five strings, omitting the sixth [E] string to play D#. Another name for D# is E♭.

D#m (E♭m)

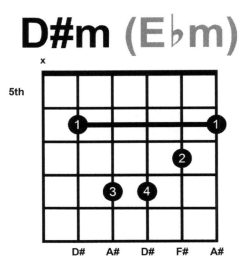

x

5th

D# A# D# F# A#

Step by Step Fingering Instructions

Begin by placing your index (1) finger as flat as you can across the sixth fret of all five strings beginning at the fifth [A] string. Omit the sixth [E] string for this chord. Next, add your middle (2) finger to the seventh fret of the second [B] string. Last, add your ring (3) finger and your pinky (4) finger to the eighth frets of the fourth [D] and third [G] strings, respectively. Once all fingers are in place you will strum only the last five strings, leaving out the sixth [E] string. Another name for D#m is E♭m.

D#m7 (E♭m7)

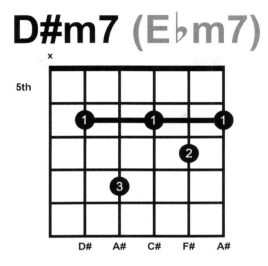

Step by Step Fingering Instructions

Begin by laying your index (1) finger as flat as you can across the sixth fret of the last five strings. Omit the sixth [E] string for this chord. Next, add your middle (2) finger to the seventh fret of the second [B] string. Last, add your ring (3) finger to the eighth fret of the third [G] string. Strum only the last five strings. Another name for D#m7 is E♭m7.

D#sus (E♭sus)

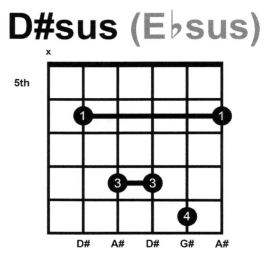

Step by Step Fingering Instructions

Begin by placing your index (1) finger on the sixth fret across the last five strings, omitting the sixth [E] string. Next, take your ring (3) finger to barre the eighth fret of the fourth [D] and third [G] strings. Last, place your pinky (4) finger on the ninth fret of the second [B] string. Strum only the last five strings, omitting the sixth [E] string to play D#sus. The other name for D#sus is E♭sus.

82

D#2 (E♭2)

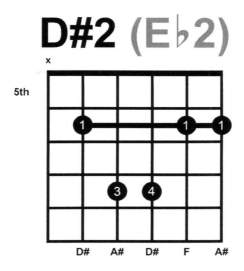

Step by Step Fingering Instructions

Start by placing your index (1) finger on the sixth fret across the bottom five strings, omitting the sixth [E] string. Last, add your ring (3) and pinky (4) fingers to the eighth frets of the fourth [D] and third [G] strings, respectively. Strum only the last five strings to produce a play D#2. The other name for D#2 is E♭2.

D#Maj7 (E♭Maj7)

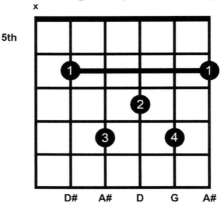

Step by Step Fingering Instructions

To begin, barre the sixth fret of fifth [A] string to the first [e] string. Next, add your ring (3) finger to the eighth fret of the fourth [D] string. Next, add your middle (2) finger to the seventh fret of the third [G] string. Finally, add your pinky (4) finger to the eighth fret of the second [B] string. Strum only the last five strings. The other name for D#Maj7 is E♭Maj7.

D#6 (E♭6)

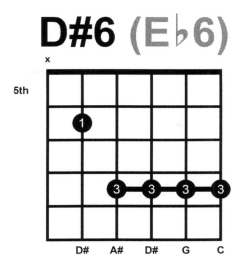

Step by Step Fingering Instructions

Begin by placing your index (1) finger on the sixth fret of the fifth [A] string. Last, barre your ring (3) finger across the eighth frets of the fourth [D], third [G], second [B], and first [e] strings. Your ring (3) finger may be difficult to keep in place at first. Strum across only the last five strings. Another name for D#6 is E♭6.

D#7 (E♭7)

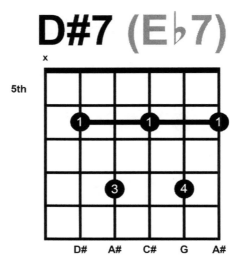

Step by Step Fingering Instructions

Begin by laying your index (1) finger across the sixth fret of the last five strings. This should be a strong barre in order to hear both the fifth [A], third [G], and first [e] strings being held down after you finish positioning each finger for this chord. Next, add your ring (3) finger onto the eighth fret of the fourth [D] string. Last, add your pinky (4) finger to the eighth fret of the second [B] string. Strum only the last five strings. Another name for D#7 is E♭7.

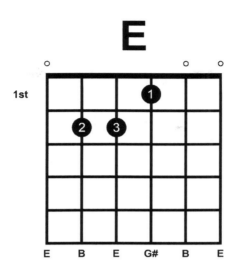

Step by Step Fingering Instructions

Begin by placing your middle (2) finger on the second fret of the fifth [A] string. Next, place your ring (3) finger onto the second fret of the fourth [D] string. Last, place your index (1) finger onto the first fret of the third [G] string. Strum all six strings to play E.

Em

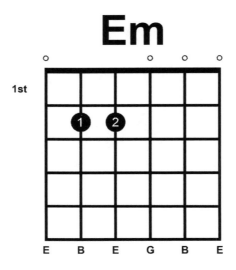

Step by Step Fingering Instructions

Place your index (1) finger onto the second fret of the fifth [A] string. Next, and finally, as this chord is easy to fret, add your middle (2) finger to the second fret of the fourth [D] string. Strum all six strings to play Em.

Em7

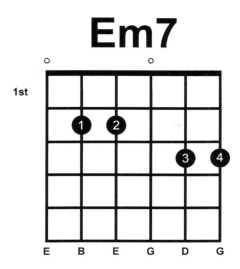

Step by Step Fingering Instructions

Place your index (1) finger and your middle (2) finger onto the second frets of the fifth [A] and fourth [D] strings, respectively. Next, add your ring (3) finger and pinky (4) finger to the third frets of the second [B] and first [e] strings. Strum all six strings for Em7.

Esus

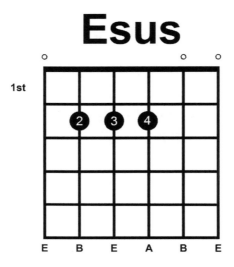

Step by Step Fingering Instructions

Begin by placing your middle (2) finger on the second fret of the fifth [A] string. Next, set your ring (3) finger onto the second fret of the fourth [D] string. Last, place your pinky (4) finger onto the second fret of the third [G] string. Strum all six strings to make Esus.

E2

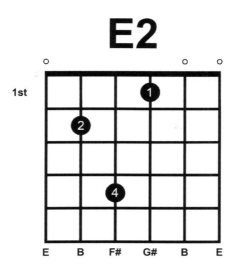

1st

E   B   F#   G#   B   E

Step by Step Fingering Instructions

Begin by placing your middle (2) finger on the second fret of the fifth [A] string. Next, place your index (1) finger onto the first fret of the third [G] string. Finally, make a pretty far stretch to place your pinky (4) finger on the fourth fret of the fourth [D] string. Strum across all six strings to play E2.

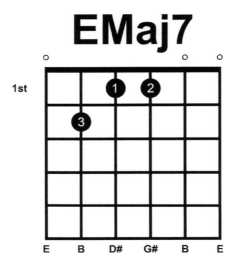

Step by Step Fingering Instructions

Begin by placing your index (1) finger on the first fret of the fourth [D] string. Next, place your middle (2) finger onto the first fret of the third [G] string. Last, place your ring (3) finger onto the second fret of the fifth [A] string. Strum all six strings to play EMaj7.

E6

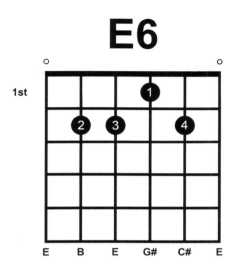

Step by Step Fingering Instructions

Start by placing your middle (2) finger on the second fret of the fifth [A] string. Next, place your ring (3) finger onto the second fret of the fourth [D] string. Continuing forward, place your index (1) finger onto the first fret of the third [G] string. Last, place your pinky (4) finger onto the second fret of the second [2] string. Strum all six strings to play an E6 chord.

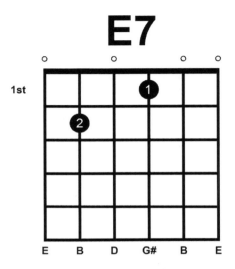

Step by Step Fingering Instructions

Begin by placing your middle (2) finger on the second fret of the fifth [A] string. place your index (1) finger onto the first fret of the third [G] string. Strum all six strings making sure to hear the open note on the fourth [D] string for E7.

F

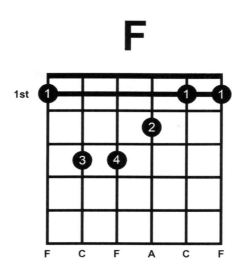

1st

F   C   F   A   C   F

Step by Step Fingering Instructions

First, lay your index (1) finger across all six strings on the first fret. You need to press down all the strings so that you can hear each note. Next, add your ring (3) and pinky (4) fingers onto the third frets of the fifth [A] and fourth [D] strings, respectively. Last, add your middle (2) finger onto the second fret of the third [G] string. Once all in place, strum across all six strings to produce an F chord. Make sure that your barre is strong and that you can hear each note that is being pressed down firmly.

Fm

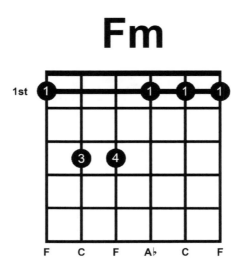

Step by Step Fingering Instructions

Begin by laying your index (1) finger across all six strings on the first fret. Next, add your ring (3) and pinky (4) fingers to the third frets of the fifth [A] and fourth [D] strings, respectively. Once each finger is in place, strum across all six strings to produce an Fm chord. Make sure to keep a strong barre on the first frets of the third [G], second [B], and first [e] strings. The minor note, "Ab", is created on the first fret of the third [G] string. Make sure you can hear that note.

Fm7

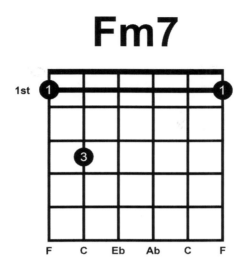

1st

F   C   Eb   Ab   C   F

Step by Step Fingering Instructions

First, lay your index (1) finger across all six strings on the first fret. Next, add your ring (3) finger to the third fret of the fifth [A] string. Once each finger is in place, strum across all six strings to produce an Fm7 chord. Make sure that you can hear the "E♭" note that is being pressed down on the first fret of the fourth [D] string. Along with the "A♭" on the third [G] string, both notes are creating the m7 in Fm7.

Fsus

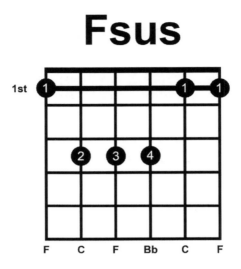

1st

F   C   F   Bb   C   F

Step by Step Fingering Instructions

First, lay your index (1) finger across all six strings on the first fret. You need to press down all the strings so that you can hear each note. Next, add your middle (2), ring (3), and pinky (4) fingers onto the third frets of the fourth [D], fifth [A] and fourth [D] strings, respectively. Once all in place, strum across all six strings to sound Fsus.

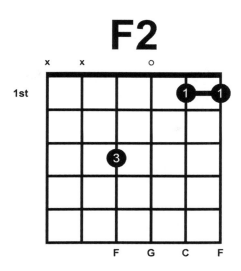

Step by Step Fingering Instructions

First, begin by placing your index (1) finger barred across both first frets of the second [B] and the first [e] strings. This barre should be as strong as possible. Make sure you can hear both notes clearly when played individually. Last, add your ring (3) finger to the third fret of the fourth [D] string. Only strum the last four strings, making sure to omit the sixth [E] and fifth [A] strings. Also, make sure that the third [G] string is left open and can be heard when you strum the F2.

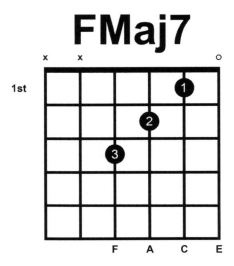

Step by Step Fingering Instructions

Begin by placing your index (1) finger onto the first fret of the second [B] string. Next, add your middle (2) finger to the second fret of the third [G] string. Last, add your ring (3) finger onto the third fret of the fourth [D] string. Strum only the last four strings to play FMaj7. Make sure to keep the first [e] string open. That "e" note makes the chord a "Maj7".

F6

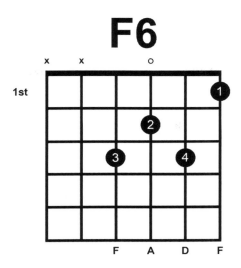

Step by Step Fingering Instructions

Begin by placing your index (1) finger onto the first fret of the first [e] string. Next, add your middle (2) finger to the second fret of the third [G] string. Then add your ring (3) finger to the third fret of the fourth [D] string. Last, add your pinky (4) finger to the third fret of the second [B] string. Strum only the last four strings to play F6.

F7

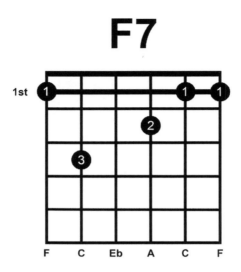

F   C   Eb   A   C   F

Step by Step Fingering Instructions

Begin by laying your index (1) finger across all six strings on the first fret. You need to press down all the strings so that you can hear each note. Next, add your ring (3) finger onto the third fret of the fifth [A] string. Last, add your middle (2) finger onto the second fret of the third [G] string. Once all in place, strum across all six strings to produce an F7 chord. Make sure you hear the fourth [D] string's note that is being pressed down by your index (1) finger. This note is the "7" in F7.

F# (G♭)

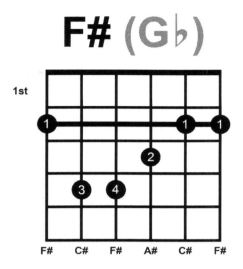

1st

F# C# F# A# C# F#

Step by Step Fingering Instructions

First, lay your index (1) finger across all six strings on the second fret. Next, add your ring (3) and pinky (4) fingers onto the fourth frets of the fifth [A] and fourth [D] strings, respectively. Finally, place your middle (2) finger onto the third fret of the third [G] string. Strum across all six strings. Another name for F# is G♭. They are one and the same.

F#m (G♭m)

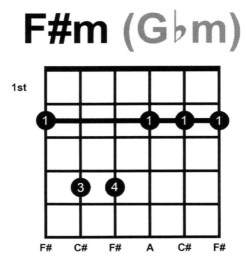

Step by Step Fingering Instructions

The first step is to lay your index (1) finger across all six strings on the second fret. Next, add your ring (3) and pinky (4) fingers on the fourth frets of the fifth [A] and fourth [D] strings, respectively. Once in place, you should be able to strum across all six strings and produce an F#m chord. It is important that you hear the second fret note on the third [G] string as that is what is making the chord a minor. The other way to say F#m is G♭m.

F#m7 (G♭m7)

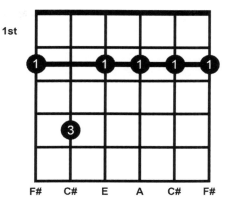

Step by Step Fingering Instructions

Begin by laying your index (1) finger across all six strings on the second fret. Next, add your ring (3) finger to the fourth fret of the fifth [A] string. Strum all six strings. It is important to make sure that the third [G] string can be heard while pressing down the second fret with your index (1) finger. That note is the *minor* note of the F#m7 chord. Your index (1) finger is also making the 7 note sound on the second fret of the fourth [D] string. Be careful to make sure you hear each note of this six string barre chord. The other name for F#m7 is G♭m7.

F#sus (G♭sus)

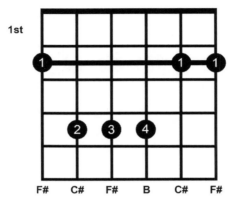

Step by Step Fingering Instructions

Start by playing your index (1) finger across all six strings on the second fret. Next, add your middle (2), ring (3), and pinky (4) fingers on the fourth frets of the fifth [A], fourth [D], and third [G] strings. Strum across all six strings. Another name for F#sus is G♭sus.

F#2 (Gb2)

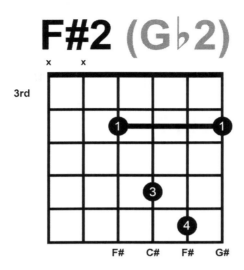

3rd

F#   C#   F#   G#

Step by Step Fingering Instructions

Begin by placing your index (1) finger across the fourth fret beginning on the fourth [D] string to the first (e) string. Omit the bottom sixth [E] and fifth [A] strings. Next, add your ring (3) finger to the sixth fret of the third [G] string. Last, add your pinky (4) finger to the seventh fret of the second [B] string. Strum only the last four strings.

F#Maj7 (G♭Maj7)

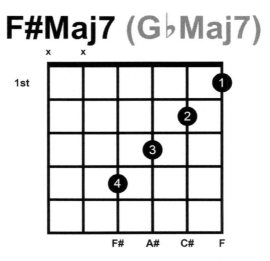

F# A# C# F

Step by Step Fingering Instructions

Start by placing your pinky (4) finger onto the fourth fret of the fourth [D] string. As close to one motion as possible, attempt to place these fingers in this order at the same time: ring (3) finger on the third fret of the third [G] string; middle (2) finger on the second fret of the second [B] string; index (1) finger on the first fret of the first [e] string. Strum only the last four strings. Another name for F#Maj7 is G♭Maj7.

F#6 (G♭6)

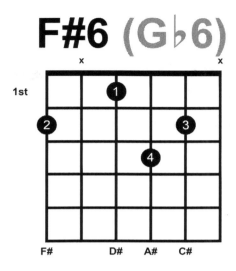

Step by Step Fingering Instructions

Start by placing your index (1) finger on the first fret of the fourth [D] string. Next, add your middle (2) finger to the second fret of the sixth [E] string. Following, add your ring (3) finger to the second fret of the second [B] string. Finally, stretch your ring (4) finger to the third fret of the third [G] string. Allow your middle (2) and ring (3) fingers to lightly touch the fifth [A] and first [e] strings, respectively. This allows those strings to be muted. Strum across all six strings to create the sound of F#6, also known as G♭6.

F#7 (G♭7)

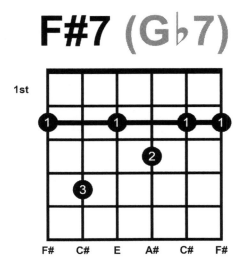

Step by Step Fingering Instructions

Begin by laying your index (1) finger across all six strings on the second fret. Now add your ring (3) finger onto the fourth fret of the fifth [A] string. Finally, place your middle (2) finger onto the third fret of the third [G] string. Strum across all six strings. It is important to hear the E note played on the fourth [D] string. This is the 7 note in F#7. Another name for F#7 is G♭7.

A Note About Diminished Chords

Why are there no diminished chords in this book?

If you've played music on the piano or are a more seasoned guitarist you may be asking why are there no diminished chords in this manual? First–In case you don't know–a diminished chord is a type of dark sounding, extremely minor chord that flattens both the third and fifth notes of a chord triad. The answer to the question above is two-fold. One, I attempted to only include mostly four, five, and six-string guitar chords. Typically a diminished chord is only three or four strings. The second reason is that diminished chords are often used as passing chords. A passing chord is one that isn't held very long and is used to pass one main chord to the next. In those cases, it's not as important to play the root note. While I know this is rather technical, I do suggest a way to use the chords in this book to serve the same passing chord–diminished–flavoring, but use a more robust chord shape. This special technique is replacing all diminished chords with 7 chords instead. It's because 7's are built using the same notes as diminished. Yes, it's complicated, but you can use 7's in this way. Below are my recommendations as to which 7 chord to use in place of its diminished counterpart.

Diminished alternatives that ARE in this book:

G7 alternatively replaces Bdim

G#7 (A♭7) alternatively replaces Cdim

A7 alternatively replaces C#dim (D♭dim)

A#7 (B♭7) alternatively replaces Ddim

B7 alternatively replaces D#dim (E♭dim)

C7 alternatively replaces Edim

C#7 (D♭7) alternatively replaces Fdim

D7 alternatively replaces F#dim (G♭dim)

D#7 (E♭7) alternatively replaces Gdim

E7 alternatively replaces G#dim (A♭dim)

F7 alternatively replaces Adim

F#7 (G♭7) alternatively replaces A#dim (B♭dim)

Closing

Recommended Resources

While this flipbook is a handy resource to keep with your guitar at all times, there are four other books in this series. I cannot recommend them highly enough.

Worship Guitar In Six Weeks

Worship Guitar In Six Weeks is a perfect primer for anyone interested in joining a worship team as a rhythm guitar player. The premise is that you really need only a few quick tools to learn before you have enough knowledge and skill to play with a group. This book teaches the parts that make up the guitar, a few important chords, how to strum, and a bit more. I recommend this book for a complete beginner. The pacing is perfect!

42 Guitar Chords Everyone Should Know

Using *42 Guitar Chords Everyone Should Know*,

you'll take a deeper dive into how guitar chords relate one to another. While the information may look similar to this book, the chords are laid out more as training exercises. For example, you'll learn how to move quickly between G to D to Em to Cadd9–each chord important for the key of G. *42 Chords* is a great next step after *Worship Guitar In Six Weeks*.

Fast Guitar Chord Transitions

One of the neatest books I've ever worked on is *Fast Guitar Chord Transitions*. Most guitar manuals will show you how to play chords. This includes finger placement, which strings to strum, and so on. In fact, this very book you have in your hands does that very thing. But, one overlooked aspect of the guitar is that transitioning between chords is just as important as knowing the chords themselves. In *Fast Guitar Chord Transitions*, I walk a guitarist through the steps of transitioning all of the most popular chord moves you'll need to know. The book is arranged based on the key of a song in which you may be playing. It's worth every penny!

Guitar Secrets Revealed

The final book in the *Guitar Authority Series* is *Guitar Secrets Revealed*. This book is for the intermediate player looking for professional level insights. Use this manual to get inside the mind of the pro. Find out how they think. You'll learn practicable–actionable–music theory that can be implemented today. Plus, find out how to use more unique guitar chord shapes that work like inversions of basic chords. All in all, this book takes a guitar player to the next level–maybe even up two levels!

BONUS: Piano Chords One and Two

While the scope of the book in your hands is for guitar players, I cannot highly recommend enough my *Piano Authority Series* of books: *Piano Chords One* and *Two*. Quickly translate everything that you know about guitar chords to the piano. You'd be amazed at how much transfers! Written much like a guitar manual, you'll learn the most important chords to play on the piano and how to play all the different versions of them. If you've ever longed to be able to play through songs on the piano and accompany yourself, these two books will help you do that. Grab a copy and see what you can accomplish!

About The Author

Why so many people learn music from Micah

The best instructors teach to the student, not to the curriculum. The curriculum serves as a vehicle for learning. It's a tool of sorts. One of the best parts of teaching music lessons–in this case, guitar chording–is the ability to help a student learn at just the right pace. I've found that my job as an educator is to always be encouraging my students to take one step more than he or she may not have taken on their own. The only thing to sort out is at which pace each student performs best.

I've been teaching guitar and piano courses for more than ten years. In fact, that's why I've written five books for guitar and two for piano to date. My emphasis has always been, and will likely always be, in commercial music. While I think classical music is worth studying, I always find myself improvising over the original melodies–even those of the greats, like Beethoven, Brahms, or Bach. It's human nature to explore or be curious and I love teaching with the mindset that the music greats of the past are like proven guides. They shouldn't always be copied, but rather those from whom to learn.

Living twenty-five miles from downtown Nashville, TN has provided myself and family privileges in music that I'm certain are not given in every town. You can't throw a stone in Nashville without hitting someone who is personally or has a family member in the music industry. Not one of us takes the Grand Ole Opry backstage tour because we all plan to be there as an artist someday. Even if we sing and play music for Jesus as Christian or worship artists, we still likely won't spend the time or money for that tour. We plan to perform on that ageless circle that lands center-stage someday ourselves.

My wife of more than ten years is glowing brighter every year. We have four kids who keep us very busy and quite exhausted! We also keep two Yorkshire Terrier dogs who I'm sure my wife would give away for less than the price of two movie tickets. I love them though.

It's an honor to help you work toward your guitar chording goals. These new chords may unlock creativity in you that has been buried deep within for years. It's time to let it out!

Blessings,

-Micah Brooks
www.micahbrooks.com
Find me on Facebook, Twitter, LinkedIn, Instagram, and Amazon.com

Connect With Micah Brooks

Signup for Micah Brooks emails to stay up to date

Subscribe to the Micah Brooks Company "Stay Connected" email list for the latest book releases. This email list is always free and intended to deliver high-value content to your inbox. Visit the link below to signup.

www.micahbrooks.com

Contact Micah

Email Micah Brooks at micahbrooks.com/contact. I want to know who you are. It's my privilege to respond to your emails personally. Please feel free to connect.

Please share this book with your friends

If you would like to share your thanks for this book, the best thing you can do is to tell a friend about *Guitar Chord Flipbook* or buy them a copy. You can also show your appreciation for this book by leaving a five star review on Amazon:

www.amazon.com

Follow Micah Brooks:

Facebook: @micahbrooksofficial
Twitter: @micahbrooksco
LinkedIn: Micah Brooks
Instagram: @micahbrooksco
Amazon: amazon.com/author/micahbrooks

If you have trouble connecting to any of these social media accounts, please visit www.micahbrooks.com.

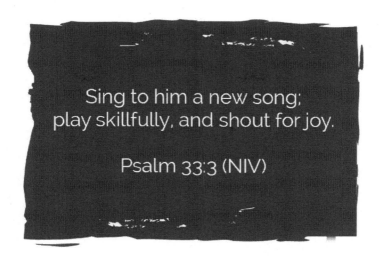

Sing to him a new song;
play skillfully, and shout for joy.

Psalm 33:3 (NIV)

Made in the USA
Las Vegas, NV
19 November 2020

11172064R00068